The Seventh Chester Book of Motets

Motets for 3 voices

Edited by Anthony G. Petti

LIST OF MOTETS

CHESTER MUSIC

Cover:
Virgin and Child in a landscape. Netherlandish School.
Presented by Queen Victoria to the National Gallery
at the Prince Consort's wish in 1863
Reproduced by courtesy of the Trustees,
The National Gallery, London.

DEUS CANTICUM NOVUM

O God, I will sing you a new song, alleluia; on the ten-stringed lyre I will play for you, alleluia. You are my God, and I shall acknowledge you and exalt you, alleluia. (Based on *Ps. 144*).

Giovanni Matteo Asola
(c. 1528 - 1609)

4

O VOS OMNES

All you who pass by, stop and see if you have seen any sorrow like my sorrow (*Lamentations*, i, 12).

Giovanni Matteo Asola
(c. 1540-1609)

MEMENTO SALUTIS AUCTOR

Remember, you who are the source of our well-being, that once you assumed
our shape by being born to a pure Virgin.
Mother of compassion, keep us from harm and receive us at the hour of our death.
Glory to you, Lord, born to the Virgin, together with the Father and the Holy
Spirit, for ever. Amen.

William Byrd
(1543-1623)

Part 2.

Part 3.

EGO FLOS CAMPI

I am the flower of the field and the lily of the valley. As a lily among thorn bushes,
so is my dear one among the maidens. As an apple tree among other trees in a wood
so is my beloved among the young men (*Song of Songs*, 2, i-iii).

Clemens non Papa
(c. 1510 - 1556)

CONFITEMINI DOMINO

Give thanks to the Lord, for he is good: for his mercy shall last for ever.
Alleluia.

Alessandro Costantini
(c.1581–c.1657)

RECORDARE DOMINE

Remember, Lord, what has happened to us: consider and see our
degradation (*Lamentations* v, 1.).

Elzéar Genet (Carpentras)
(c. 1470–1548)

SEDERUNT IN TERRA

The elders of the daughter of Zion sat upon the ground and were silent: they scattered ashes on their heads; the daughters of Jerusalem have wrapped themselves in sackcloth; the daughters of Juda have bowed their heads to the ground (*Lamentations*, ii, 10).

Elzéar Genet (Carpentras)
(c.1470-1548)

ADORAMUS TE CHRISTE

We adore you, O Christ, and we bless you, because by your holy cross you
have redeemed the world. Have mercy on us, Lord.

Orlandus Lassus
(1532-1594)

IN PACE

Peacefully I immediately fall asleep and lie at rest, because you alone, Lord,
have given me security. (*Ps. 4* ix–x)

Orlandus Lassus
(1532–1594)

AVE MARIA

Hail Mary, full of grace, the Lord is with thee, blessed art thou among
women, and blessed is the fruit of thy womb, Jesus. Holy Mary, mother
of God, pray for us sinners now and at the hour of our death. Amen.

Claudio Monteverdi
(1567 - 1643)

LAUDA SION

Sion, praise your Saviour, praise your king and shepherd in hymns and songs.
Strive to honour him with all your power; for he excels beyond all exaltation,
neither can praise ever be sufficient. Good shepherd, true bread, O Jesus,
have mercy on us. Feed us, tend us, make us to enjoy grace in the land of the
living. (St. Thomas Aquinas, 1225-74)

Claudio Monteverdi
(1567 - 1643)

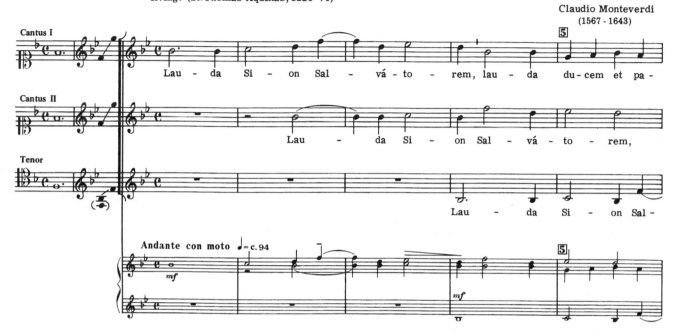

DOMINE DEUS

Lord, God, Lamb of God, Son of the Father.

Cristóbal Morales
(c.1500–1553)

IN DIE TRIBULATIONIS

In my hour of need I have called to you because you listen to me.
None of the gods is comparable to you, Lord, and no achievements are like
yours. You have caused the people of every race to come and adore you,
Lord, and they will glorify your name! For you alone are great and work
wonders; you alone are God (*Ps. 86*, vi–ix).

Cristóbal Morales
(c. 1500–1553)

JESU REX ADMIRABILIS

Jesus, wonderful king and noble conqueror,
Inexpressible sweetness, totally desired.

Remain with us, Lord, and illuminate us by your light,
The darkness of the mind being driven out, fill the world with sweetness.

G. P. da Palestrina
(1525–1594)

* In the original there is only a single *longa* in each part and no underlay.
It is therefore doubtful whether *Amen* is intended, but custom usually includes it.

TUA JESU DILECTIO

1. Love of you, Jesus, is a fulfilling pleasure to the mind:
   It satisfies without cloying, and increases desire.

2. Those who taste of you hunger for more, those who drink thirst for more:
   Their only desire is the Jesus they love. Amen.

G. P. da Palestrina
(1525-1594)

* See note at end of preceding motet.

EDITOR'S NOTES

The aim of this present series is to make more readily available a comprehensive body of Latin motets from the Renaissance and Early Baroque periods, combining the inclusion of old favourites with the provision of lesser known or hitherto unpublished works. Generally speaking, all the pieces are within the scope of the reasonably able choir. They also encompass a fair selection from the liturgical year as a guide for use both in church and in the concert hall when performing choirs wish to present their programme according to a theme or a particular season.

The editor has endeavoured to preserve a balance between a critical and performing edition. The motets are, where necessary, transposed into the most practical performing keys, are barred, fully underlaid and provided with breathing marks. They also have a reduction either as a rehearsal aid or as a form of accompaniment, since at least some of the works of the later period were clearly intended to be reinforced by a continuo. Editorial tempi and dynamics are supplied only in the reduction, leaving choirmasters free to supply their own in the light of their interpretation of a given piece, vocal resources and the acoustics. The vocal range is given at the beginning of each motet. Also provided are a translation of every text and a table of use.

As an aid to musicologists, the motets are transcribed, wherever possible, from the most authoritative sources, and the original clefs, signatures and note values are given at the beginning and wherever they change during the course of a piece. Ligatures are indicated by slurs, editorial accidentals are placed above the stave, and the underlay is shown in italics when it expands a ditto sign, or in square brackets when it is entirely editorial. Where the original contains a basso continuo this is included as the bass line of the reduction. Figurings are not included, however , because they are extremely sparse, and do not normally indicate any more than the harmony already provided by the vocal parts. Finally, each volume includes a brief introduction concerning the scope of the edition, with notes on the composers, the motets and the sources, together with a list of editorial emendations and alterations, if any.

This volume contains fifteen motets gathered from the works of nine composers. The collection is designed for equal female or boys' voices (SSA) but can readily be used by equal male voices (TTB) providing the basses can read from the G clef. Various other combinations can be used, including mixed voices, as set out in the appropriate table at the end of these notes.

Motets for three voices are far more common for the Renaissance and Early Baroque periods than is generally supposed, as can easily be ascertained merely by glancing through a chronological list of published collections of sacred music (RISM, *Recueils imprimés xvi-xvii siècles,* 1960). In the early 16th century, the habit of composing three-part motets seems to be a continuation of late medieval practice, and the same applies to secular music: witness the bulk of vocal music performed at the court of Henry VIII. Towards the end of the century, three-part motets and masses of varying degrees of polyphonic complexity are readily found, as are three-part canzonets; and in the early 17th century, the Baroque vogue for the basso continuo favours not only polychoral works, but also the more intimate groups of one, two and three voices. Further, it should be remembered that the Renaissance also produced one of the finest three-part sacred works ever written: Byrd's *Mass for Three Voices.* On the other hand, relatively few of the major Renaissance composers wrote more than a handful of three-part motets, though some, like Palestrina, used three voices in sections of larger works, most notably, in the *Benedictus* section of the Mass.

The first two pieces in this collection are by Giovanni Matteo (or Giammateo) Asola, who was born in Verona around 1528. He trained for the priesthood at the college of the Canons Regular near Venice, and thereafter spent much of his life in Venice, where he published several collections of music, including madrigals, a volume of masses and two books of Psalms, one for eight voices and one for six. He was chapel master at Treviso briefly and then at Vicenza. Most of his sacred music, including about forty masses, seems to have been written during the years he occupied the Vicenza post. His final years were spent as a chaplain in Venice. He died in 1607. Recent opinion suggests that Asola is more of a traditionalist than has been previously stated, and that he writes somewhat in the style of Palestrina. That he was one of the first to use a basso continuo is now doubted, though he must have intended accompaniment for at least some of his three-part works. The Asola motets included here both come from three-part collections, copies of which are housed in the Liceo Musicale, Bologna. *Deus canticum novum* is to be found in *Missae duodecimque sacrae laudes 3 vocibus concinendae* (2nd impression, Venice, 1588). A later edition (1620) includes a basso continuo (reproduced here in the bass) but there is no evidence that it was supplied or authorized by Asola. The motet is a lively and brisk, yet smooth treatment of the text. The progressions are enterprisingly harmonic rather than modal, despite the impression of Hypodorian mode at the beginning, and the style is free, with a mixture of the chordal and compact fugal imitation. The sections are clearly delineated and do not overlap. Word-painting is remarkably sparse for such a text (apart from the rising phrases for "psallam") and the underlay is treated monosyllabically. As against this economy, the text phrases are frequently reiterated, often in identical melodic forms, in a bold use of rhetorical repetition, this giving the work a sufficient sense of expansiveness and continuity.

The *O vos omnes* is contained in *Lamentationes, Improperia et aliae sacrae laudes, tribus vocibus,* Venice, 1588. Like most settings of the text, it is slow-moving, compact and mainly homophonic, though there is a brief descending fugal passage towards the end for "Sicut dolor" (bars 23ff.). As with *Deus canticum novum,* there is mainly a feeling for keys with A minor predominating (in the present transposition). Worthy to bear comparison with the settings of Jaquet of Mantua, Victoria, Croce and Felice Anerio (with all of which it has some affinities), the piece has poignancy and a fine sense of contours, with especially effective use of paired upper parts, usually in close similar motion. It should be noted that, contrary to usual practice, the versicle "Attendite" is not included.

Three-part motets seem to have been least popular with the English composers of the 16th century. Even William Byrd, who was one of the most prolific, wrote comparatively few: thirteen in all, eleven of which were published in his *Gradualia,* Book One (copy of 1610 edition in the British Library). *Memento salutis auctor* (no. 3 of the eleven) is a hymn of great beauty and technical mastery, and is so well extended and sustained that each of its three sections (one for each stanza) could serve as a separate motet. The writing is remarkably simple for Byrd, with none of the rhythmic intricacy of his three-part *Mass*, though echoing one of its phrases: "cum sancto spiritu" of the *Gloria,* at a juncture where the text, too, is similar: "cum Patre et Sancto Spiritu" (bars 60ff.). As with Asola, the feeling is less for the Aeolian mode than for the minor (here A, originally D), because of the consistently raised leading note. As the supplication grows in optimism, C♯ begins to be heard and occasionally F♯ and G♯, so that by the end of the doxology, the key is triumphantly A major. For Parts One and Two, the treatment is similar to that of a Tallis hymn: gentle and in a compact and nearly homphonic style, with relatively few text repetitions. By contrast, Part Three launches into an assertive and animated fugue of praise, and climaxes with a swift-moving, rhythmic and syncopated "amen," which seems to have antecedents in the works of Byrd's great predecessor, John Taverner (e.g., the "venit" of *Audivi, Second Book of Chester Motets,* p. 37).

The next motet, *Ego flos campi,* is item 7 of *Premier livre du recueil des fleurs produictes de la divine musique a trois parties.* Louvain, 1560 (transcribed from the copy in the Bayerische Staatsbibliothek, Munich). It contains the exquisite melodic beauty and fine melding of polyphonic strands typical of most of the other sacred music of Clemens non Papa (biographical details in *Fifth Book of Chester Motets*). The very opening, with its well-aired fugue, has a delicacy and lyricism which one normally attributes to the best of Palestrina, and it is hard not to feel that Palestrina was influenced in these respects by the Flemish master. The musical phrases respond well to the personal, emotive and mystical quality of the poetry. The lines are mellifluous without cloying, natural and easy without being predictable. In the usual Clemens style (found also in Palestrina), each section gradually flowers, and comes to a satisfactory climax and cadence before giving way to the succeeding section. The harmony relies little on suspensions and is predominantly in the bright Ionian mode, though ending in the dominant, suggestive of the Mixolydian mode. That Clemens felt affinity to this type of liturgical text is indicated by his providing a seven-part setting also.

With Alessandro Costantini (c. 1581-c.1657) we come to the latest of the composers and possibly the least known. Brother of a more celebrated composer, Fabio, he was an accomplished organist, occupying many important posts in Rome, and eventually becoming organist at St. Peter's on the death of Frescobaldi in 1643. His motet, *Confitemini Domino,* the only one in this collection originally supplied with a basso continuo, is no. 19 of *Motecta singulis, binis, ternisque vocibus, cum basso ad organum concinenda, liber primus,*Rome, 1616 (copy in British Library). The setting is for three tenors (a combination favoured by Early Baroque composers including Monteverdi cf. his *Duo Seraphim* from the *Vespers*), but works well for upper voices too. The motet is buoyant, extrovert and straight-forward, though presumably would have been highly ornamented when sung by solo voices. As if looking back to Asola, it combines chordal unity at the beginning with brief fugues later on (e.g. at "misericordia" and "alleluia"). To emphasize the joy of the piece it moves into quick triple time for the final section. It is also markedly harmonic, for it quickly dispels the notion of a Hypomixolydian mode by the swift and frequent introduction of F♯ to establish G major as the prevailing key, and securely modulates into the related keys of D major and A major. Modulation grows more adventurous and subtle by the time of the "alleluia" section, the rhythm also becoming a little more sophisticated. Word accentuation, as might be expected, is meticulously paralleled by the musical ictus.

Almost as little known as Costantini is Elezéar Genet (c. 1470-1548), the earliest composer represented here. He was born at Carpentras, near Avignon, and was commonly known as Carpentras, a custom which also explains Palestrina's appellation. Carpentras took holy orders at Avignon. In 1508 he became a singer in the Papal Chapel under Julius II, but quickly returned to France to join the court of Louis XII. His most important position was as chapel master for Leo X (1514-21), after which he spent the remainder of his life back in Avignon (see further, Albert Seay, *Elziani Geneti opera omnia,* C.M.M., 58). Carpentras' compositions include masses, hymns and magnificats. His best known work seems to have been the *Lamentations,* which were cherished by the Papal Chapel, and it is therefore from these that the present two pieces are taken (*Liber Lamentationum Hieremiae Prophetae,* Avignon, 1532). The printed text (Bibliothèque Nationale, Paris) has been preferred for this transcription, because it seems more accurate than the manuscript versions. The two motets indicate some of the variety of treatment which Carpentras is capable of in the *Lamentations,* and both show his free-ranging use of modes and his penchant for suspended and ornamented cadences, usually featuring 9/8 or 7/6 chords. *Recordare* begins in a slow, ascending fugue of supplication between the outer parts, and keeps the voices staggered almost throughout. The melodic line moves mainly by step, and the melismas are usually ascending or descending scale passages (e.g., "intuere" and "respice"), so that the quick succession of fourth leaps for "opprobrium" are all the more striking in that strongly emotive passage. By contrast with *Recordare,* the second piece, *Sederunt in terra,* is much more homophonic, resembling in places the *falsobordone* treatment of other sections of the *Lamentations.* Voice pairings are common, and there is a climactic use of text repetition. Towards the end, melismas are introduced as if both to intensify and give release to the expression of sorrow.

The versatile Orlandus Lassus (biographical details in *Fifth Book of Chester Motets*) wrote about two dozen three-part motets, all contained in *Magnum Opus Musicum,* Munich, 1604 (copy in the British Library, from which the two pieces published there were transcribed). This version of the *Adoramus te Christe* (no. 43) is the more famous of two three-part settings which Lassus provided for this popular text. Set in the transposed Hypoionian mode, it is a masterly combination of melodic smoothness and structural unity, and perfectly matches the music to the mood and meaning of the words. There is a very effective interlacing and crossing of parts, especially in the canons for "et benedicimus" and "quia per tuam sanctam crucem". The climax of "redemisti" is triumphantly achieved in the G major chord, and the piece comes to rest very gently in the superb dying fall of the final "miserere nobis". *In pace* (no. 47) is also set in the Hypoionian mode, and strikes a fine balance between an almost soporific canon descending the triad for "In pace", and a sprightly and syncopated "singulariter" in the middle section (presumably as a means of expressing God's uniqueness). To conclude the piece there is an expansive, undulating, but controlled canon conveying the happy reassurance of "constituisti".

The next two pieces are by an even more versatile and brilliant composer than Lassus: Claudio Monteverdi. Born the son of a doctor in 1567, Monteverdi began his career as a choirboy in his native Cremona. In 1590 he entered the service of the Duke of Mantua, becoming his master of music in 1602. He quarrelled with the new Duke, Francesco Gonzaga, in 1612 and was dismissed. However, the following year he was appointed master of the music at St. Mark's, Venice, one of the most coveted posts in Europe, and remained in office until his death in 1643. Monteverdi's output is vast, and includes many books of madrigals in diverse styles, but always with the music securely married to the words; a large quantity of sacred music, some of it polyphonic but most of it in Early Baroque style; and several operas, which are among the earliest and most successful in this genre. The present pieces are from Monteverdi's juvenilia, being part of a collection of three-part motets he published in 1582, when he was only fifteen (*Sacrae cantiunculae tribus vocibus*, Venice, copy in the Archivio Capitolare, Archivio della Chiesa Collegiata, Castello Arquato, Italy). As the title of the collection suggests, the motets are unpretentious, melodic and very lighthearted. They do not, as might be expected, attempt a Venetian Early Baroque style, but are traditional, and somewhat in the style of his teacher, Ingegneri, and of the school of Palestrina. *Ave Maria* (no. 7 in the collection) is suitably delicate and lyrical, with the use of equal cantus lines to increase the impression of lightness. The fugal writing is controlled, being neither prolix nor congested, and the piece remains firmly in the Ionian mode. An especially delightful feature is the opening canon, which is slightly reminiscent of the beginning of the Josquin *Ave Maria*. The second Monteverdi motet, *Lauda Sion* (no. 22) is in the Palestrina tradition in general style. It even uses slow triple time for the "Bone Pastor" section as in the Palestrina settings, and selects the same three stanzas (1, 2, 23) from the twenty four of the original Aquinas hymn as the Palestria four-part setting. On the other hand, unlike the Palestrina settings, Monteverdi's owes little or nothing to the plainsong melody and is continuously polyphonic, maintaining, as in the *Ave Maria*, a delicate canon or fugue throughout. The mode, once again, is Ionian, with a suspicion of Hypoionian.

Cristóbal Morales (see *Third Chester Book of Motets* for biographical details) wrote little for three voices, but the extant pieces proved so popular that some of them were frequently anthologized, *In die tribulationis* being published four times. *Domine Deus,* the first Morales piece, is item 20 of the anthology, *Libro secondo de li motetti a tre voce,* Venice, 1549 (copy in the British Library). The text, an excerpt from the *Gloria,* seems to have been frequently selected as a motet, and the anthology contains a setting of it by another composer (item 24). The piece falls into two main but overlapping sections, and presents a set of sequential climactic fugues. The concept is simple, the progressions are effortless, and the general sense of symmetry is very pleasing. *In die tribulationis* (transcribed from the British Library copy of *Variorum linguarum tricinia,* Nuremberg, 1560) is a much longer, more varied and more thoughtful work. It has a sinuous beauty, and makes expressive use of descending six-three chords, high-lying pairings ("tu es Deus solus") and brief appropriate passages of homophony ("et adorabunt"). As the text becomes tranquil, so does the mode move from Hypoaeolian to Ionian, while the Phrygian cadence with which the work ends seems markedly positive rather than giving a sense of irresolution. In this respect, it is useful to contrast this motet with Palestrina's *Super flumina,* which in some ways is markedly similar, especially in its pattern of fugues and even in the opening phrase in the bass.

Finally, with Palestrina (biographical details in the *First Chester Book of Motets*) we come to two of the briefest yet most effective of all 16th century three-part motets. The only two extant examples of completely independent three-part motets by Palestrina, they are both settings of two stanzas from St. Bernard's hymn, *Jesu dulcis memoria,* and both are contained in the anthology, *Diletto Spirituale,* Rome 1586, (Liceo Musical, Bologna). *Jesu rex admirabilis* is a masterpiece of simplicity, though it has a few subtle modulations, moving from Dorian to Aeolian and Ionian. It is homophonic until almost the end, and concentrates on providing a well-punctuated, beautiful melody. *Tua Jesu dilectio* is obviously a companion piece and is cast in the same mould. While it has not quite the same attractiveness of melody and harmonic appeal, it seems to have an even greater tenderness of utterance.

Anthony Petti, April 1979

Table of suggested downward transpositions

	SAT	ATBar	TTB	TBarB	BarBB
Deus canticum	tone-4th	5th-8ve	8ve	8ve-9th	———
O vos omnes	tone-4th	4th-8ve	8ve	8ve-9th	9th-11th
Memento salus	same-tone	5th-8ve	8ve	8ve-9th	———
Ego flos campi	tone-4th	6th-8ve	8ve	8ve-9th	———
Confitemini	tone-4th	6th-8ve	8ve	8ve-10th	9th-12th
Recordare	3rd-4th	7th-8ve	8ve-9th	9th-11th	10th-12th
Sederunt	4th-5th	8ve-9th	8ve-10th	10th-12th	12th
Adoramus	4th	———	8ve	8ve-9th	9th-12th
In pace	———	———	8ve	8ve-9th	9th-11th
Ave Maria	4th	8ve	8ve-10th	———	———
Lauda Sion	———	8ve	8ve	———	———
Domine Deus	4th	8ve-9th	8ve-9th	———	———
In die tribulationis	3rd	8ve	8ve-9th	9th	10th
Jesu rex	same-3rd	7th-8ve	8ve	8ve-9th	———
Tua Jesu	———	8ve	8ve	———	———

Table of use according to the Tridentine Rite

Motet	Liturgical source	Seasonal or festal use
Deus canticum	Vesper psalm	General
O vos omnes	Responsory, 2nd nocturn, matins, Holy Saturday	Holy Week, Lent
Memento salus	Extract Hymn, vespers, Christmas; Little Office of Virgin (old Office)	Christmas, Blessed Virgin
Ego flos campi	Office of the Blessed Virgin	Blessed Virgin
Confitemini	Antiphon, vespers	General
Recordare	3rd lesson, 1st nocturn, matins, Holy Saturday	Holy Week, Lent
Sederunt	1st lesson, 1st nocturn, matins, Good Friday	Holy Week, Lent
Adoramus	Antiphon, Good Friday	Holy Week, Lent, general
In pace	Psalm, compline; antiphon, Holy Saturday	Evening service
Ave Maria	Antiphon of Blessed Virgin	Blessed Virgin, Advent, Annunciation
Lauda Sion	Sequence, Corpus Christi	Blessed Sacrament
Domine Deus	Gloria of the Mass	Christ, general
In die tribulationis	Psalm, compline	General, Lent
Jesu rex	Hymn, matins of Holy Name	Christ, Christmas, Easter, Ascension
Tua Jesu	Hymn, Office of Holy Name	Christ, Christmas, Easter, Ascension

Printed in EU